PHYSICAL SCIENCE IN DEPTH

FORCES AND MOTION

David L. Dreier

Heinemann Library
Chicago, Illinois

Produced for Heinemann Library by White-Thomson Publishing Ltd.
Illustrations: Kerry Flaherty
Photo Research: Amy Sparks
Production: Duncan Gilbert
Printed and bound in China by South China Printing Company Ltd.

12 11 10 09 08
10 9 8 7 6 5 4 3 2 1

Library of Congress Cataloging-in-Publication Data
Dreier, David Louis.
  Forces and motion / Dave Dreier.
      p. cm. — (Physical science in depth)
  Includes bibliographical references and index.
  ISBN 978-1-4034-9923-3 (library binding - hardcover)
  ISBN 978-1-4034-9931-8 (pbk.)
  1. Force and energy—Juvenile literature. 2. Motion—Juvenile literature.
I. Title.
  QC73.4.D74 2008
  531'.11—dc22   2007006273

Acknowledgments
The author and publishers are grateful to the following for permission to reproduce copyrighted
material: Alamy **pp. 28** (Kunst and Scheidulin), **46** (John Powell Photographer), **56** (Pixonnet.com),
57 (f1 online); Corbis **pp. 11** (Pete Stone), **14** (Max Rossi/Reuters), **15** (Duomo), **30** (Steve Chenn),
33 (Jim Sugar), **42** (Al Francekevich), **45** (Oliver Weiken/epa), **51** (Karl Staedele/dpa),
53 (Mike Watson Images), **54** (Ole Graf/zefa); Getty Images **p. 24** (Gerard Fritz); iStockphoto.com
title page (Dirk Freder), **pp. 4, 5** (Matthew Cole), **7** (Matt Duncan), **12** (S. Greg Panosian),
16 (Lawrence Sawyer), **23** (Dirk Freder), **25** (Stephan Hoerold), **35, 50** (Doug Sims), **52,**
55t (Ericsphotography), **55b** (Sean Gray); NASA **pp. 21, 36** (all), **39, 41, 58**; Photolibrary
p. 48 (Mark Deeble & Victoria Stone); Rice University **p. 59** (Y. Shirai); Science Photo Library
pp. 13 (Andrew Lambert Photography), **29** (Charles D. Winters), **43** (Jan Hinsch).

Cover photograph of a snowboarder is reproduced with permission of Corbis/Mike Chew.

Every effort has been made to contact copyright holders of any material reproduced in this book.
Any omissions will be rectified in subsequent printings if notice is given to the publisher.

The publishers would like to thank Ann and Patrick Fullick, Timothy Griffin, and Barbara Bakowski
for their assistance in the preparation of this book.

Contents

Words printed in the text in bold, **like this**,
are explained in the Glossary.

A World of Motion

Without **motion**, nothing would happen. Motion—the movement of things from one place to another—gives life to our world. We see motion everywhere we look: people working, children playing, traffic flowing. We see machines doing the world's work—tearing up streets, moving heavy objects, constructing huge buildings. Overhead, airplanes soar high above the clouds.

Every movement you see was produced by some sort of **force**. Think of a force as a push or a pull. A force is anything that sets an object in motion or changes the **speed** or direction of its motion. At least it *can* do that unless another force of equal or greater strength opposes it. You can push as hard as you want against a large, heavy boulder, but it will not move. You simply do not have enough strength to move it. Just by pushing against it, though, you exerted a force.

A force can also change the shape of an object. For example, if you flatten a lump of clay with your hands, you have used force on the clay. In this book, we will concentrate on forces that produce motion.

An amusement park is full of motion. All motions are produced by forces.

TWO KINDS OF FORCES

There are two main kinds of forces we experience in our daily lives—those that require touching and those that do not.

Most forces require touching, or physical contact. These kinds of forces are called **contact forces**, or mechanical forces. Think about that boulder again. Even if you had the strength of Superman, you would not be able to move the boulder without touching it. You would have to press your hands against it and push hard. Or you could tie a heavy rope around it and pull it. Either way, you would have to be in physical contact with the boulder. Think of all the motions you make every day, and you will realize how many require touching. For example, you cannot open a drawer without pulling on it. And you cannot close it again without pushing on it.

Some forces do not require touching. These are called noncontact forces. One such force is **magnetism**. If you hold a magnet close to a pile of paper clips, a few of the clips will jump up and become attached to the magnet. The magnet exerts a force on the paper clips across an open space.

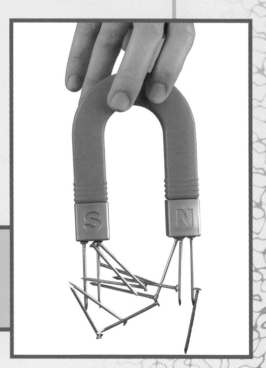

Another force that acts across open spaces is **gravity**. Gravity is the force that causes things to fall to the ground. We will explore gravity in detail later in the book.

Not all forces require contact. A small magnet can exert a force across an open space to pick up nails.

The Four Fundamental Forces

Four fundamental forces control the universe. Those forces are the **strong nuclear force**, the **weak nuclear force**, gravity, and the **electromagnetic force**. The nuclear forces play no role in everyday life. Gravity and electromagnetism, however, play a very large role. The electromagnetic force produces all the forces that involve physical contact—the mechanical pushes and pulls that are not due to gravity.

THE STRONG AND WEAK NUCLEAR FORCES

The nuclear forces play a role in processes involving the **nucleus**, or center, of **atoms**. Atoms are the smallest units of substances called **elements**. Gold and carbon are examples of elements. The smallest possible bit of gold is an atom of gold.

The strong nuclear force holds the nucleus of the atom together. The nucleus of an atom consists of tiny particles called **protons** and **neutrons**. Protons carry a positive electric charge. Neutrons are neutral—they have no electric charge. Charges of the same kind repel each other. Without the strong nuclear force to hold them together, the protons in a nucleus would fly apart.

Did you know...?

Gravity is by far the weakest of the four fundamental forces. The electromagnetic force between a proton and an electron is more than a trillion trillion trillion times stronger than the gravitational force between them. A small magnet is strong enough to hold paper clips against the downward gravitational pull of Earth's **mass**.

Gravity pulls a dropped lightbulb to the ground, causing it to shatter. Without the pull of gravity, the lightbulb would simply float in the air.

The weak nuclear force causes radioactive decay in atoms. In radioactive decay, an element breaks down into a different element. Like the strong force, the weak force operates only within tiny distances in the nucleus of atoms.

GRAVITY

Gravity is a force of attraction between all objects. The gravity of an object is determined by its mass—the amount of matter it contains. The more mass an object has, the stronger its gravitational pull on other objects. The Sun, for example, has a huge amount of mass, so it has a very large gravitation pull. Two people have a very small gravitational attraction to each other. The attraction is so tiny that it is not noticeable. People are much more attracted by the gravity of Earth, which has far more mass than a person does.

Earth's gravity pulls on everything. It is because of Earth's gravity that you can jump only a few feet into the air before falling back to the ground. Even a bullet fired high into the air is drawn speeding back to Earth. Only powerful rockets can escape from our planet's gravity.

Earth itself, along with all the other planets in the **solar system**, is held in **orbit** around the Sun by the Sun's immense gravity. All objects in the universe exert a gravitational pull on all other objects. However, the attraction between two objects becomes steadily weaker the farther apart they are.

THE ELECTROMAGNETIC FORCE

Electricity and magnetism are closely related. They are both part of a force known as the electromagnetic force, or electromagnetism. The electromagnetic force is caused by the electric charges carried by particles in atoms—protons and **electrons**. Electrons are particles that whirl around outside the nucleus. They have a negative electric charge, which is opposite to the positive charge carried by protons.

Positive and negative charges are attracted to each other, but charges of the same type repel each other. Complete atoms have an equal number of electrons and protons. That balance makes matter electrically neutral, so we do not feel the electromagnetic force—even though it is much stronger than gravity.

Atoms are the basic units of matter. An atom consists of a positively charged nucleus surrounded by negatively charged particles called electrons. The nucleus is composed of two kinds of particles: protons, which have a positive charge, and neutrons, which have no electric charge.

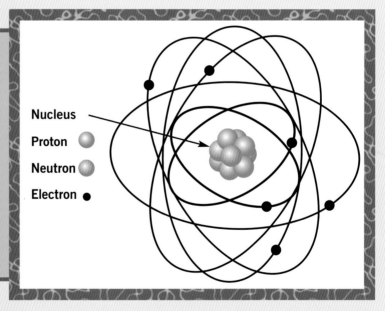

Nucleus

Proton

Neutron

Electron

The electromagnetic force does make itself visible, however. The electricity that lights our homes and powers our factories comes from this force. When you use a magnet, you are also seeing the electromagnetic force at work. Magnetism is caused by the lining up of atoms in certain materials, such as iron. The alignment of the atoms creates a magnetic field around them.

SCIENCE PIONEERS Joseph John Thompson: Discovering the Electron

Scientists could not fully explain the electromagnetic force until they first understood the structure of the atom. In 1871, the Irish physicist G. Johnstone Stoney (1826–1911) predicted the existence of the electron. British physicist Joseph John Thompson (1856–1940) confirmed it in 1897. In later years, researchers learned that almost all electromagnetic activity involves the movement of electrons.

Atoms join to form **molecules** by sharing electrons. All chemical reactions involve the making or breaking of electron bonds between atoms. It is these whirling electrons that make a rock, a chair, or any other hard object feel solid. An atom's electrons form a barrier around the nucleus. This barrier makes it impossible for one atom to force its way into another atom. To understand this, think how impossible it would be for two spinning airplane propellers to push through each other. Likewise, no matter how hard you try, you cannot push your finger into a rock.

The electromagnetic force makes mechanical forces possible. When we push on that boulder, for example, our muscles release **energy** through the chemical reactions made possible by the electromagnetic force. In the same way, many of the machines we use to move things burn fuels for energy. Therefore, almost all forces we experience in the everyday world are made possible by the electromagnetic force.

Did you know...?

You can push your finger into a gas or a liquid because the atoms or molecules are moving around loosely. With these substances, you are pushing your finger *between* the atoms or molecules.

The Basics of Everyday Forces

Forces have both a size and a direction. When you push someone on a swing, for example, you can push hard or softly. You can push the swing straight or off at an angle. Scientists call any measurement that has both a size and a direction a **vector quantity**. Forces are vector quantities.

The size of a force can be expressed in several units. The most common unit of force is called the **newton**, named for the famous British scientist Sir Isaac Newton (1642–1727). The newton is a unit in the metric system. One newton is equal to about one-tenth of a kilogram. A newton is approximately the **weight** of an apple. Weight is a type of force. But any kind of push or pull, not just a weight, can be expressed in newtons.

It is not enough, though, to say that an object is exerting a force of, say, 20 newtons. Because forces are vector quantities, they have both a size and a direction. So you must tell in which direction that force is acting. Twenty newtons downward, for example, would be a complete description of the force.

CONCURRENT AND RESULTANT FORCES

An object usually has more than one force acting on it at any time. For example, a motorboat moving upstream on a river is being pushed ahead by the force of its motor and slowed by the force of the water. Multiple forces such as these are called **concurrent forces**. These forces produce a single net, or remaining, force called the **resultant force**. The resultant force is the sum of all the concurrent forces. The resultant force of the motorboat would be the amount of force pushing the boat forward after the opposing force of the water is figured in.

BALANCED AND UNBALANCED FORCES

If the resultant force of a set of concurrent forces is zero, the concurrent forces are said to be balanced. When **balanced forces** act on something, there is no change of motion. If the concurrent forces are **unbalanced**, the resultant force is not zero—so the movement of the object changes.

Imagine two teams taking part in a tug-of-war. Both sides are pulling hard on a rope. A flag, marking the center of the rope, hangs over a line drawn on the ground. Both groups are trying to pull the flag toward their side. They are exerting great force in opposite directions. The object being acted on is the rope. The two groups are evenly matched. Neither side budges. The forces they are exerting are balanced, so the resultant force is zero. An object being acted on by balanced forces—the rope, in this case—is said to be in **equilibrium**.

Suddenly, one side gets the advantage. The forces are now unbalanced. The flag moves away from the line and toward the stronger group. Finally, the other side gives up and lets go of the rope. Their opposing force is now completely gone. The rope flies over to the winning side.

In this tug-of-war, the forces being exerted by the two teams are unbalanced. The flag is closer to the team in white shirts, which is exerting more force than its opponent.

CASE STUDY Balanced Forces in Construction

It is vital for all forces in bridges and other large structures to be in balance. Large structures are made with many heavy materials, such as steel and concrete. Gravity is trying to pull all those materials to the ground. For a structure to stand, it must support its own weight. It must also be able to withstand any other forces it might be exposed to, such as high winds. If the forces on a structure become unbalanced, the structure may collapse.

Suspension bridges use heavy vertical cables to support a roadway across the bridge. The cables are connected to even heavier cables that are draped over two high towers. Those cables are fastened to huge concrete blocks, called anchorages, at the ends of the bridge. A well-constructed bridge supports its own weight, the weight of hundreds of vehicles, and sideways forces caused by strong winds and water currents.

At one time, the Golden Gate Bridge in San Francisco was the longest suspension bridge in the world. The two tall towers support most of the bridge's weight—and the weight of the 40 million vehicles that travel the bridge's roadway each year.

MEASURING FORCES

There are many ways to measure forces. You make a force measurement every time you step on a bathroom scale. Your body exerts a downward force on the scale, and that force is shown in pounds or kilograms.

A forcemeter is a common laboratory instrument for measuring weights or other pulls. A forcemeter has a spring and a hook attached to a vertical scale. A weight can be attached to the hook, or it can be pulled by another force. A person can pull on the hook and see how much force he or she is exerting. A forcemeter is sometimes called a newton meter because the instrument's scale is usually marked off in newtons.

STRAIN GAUGES

Another commonly used force-measuring instrument is the strain gauge. When metals or other materials are subjected to forces, they can stretch or bend. The strain gauge detects such changes, even when they are very small, and converts the information into an electrical signal. As the strain on a material increases, the electrical signal gets stronger.

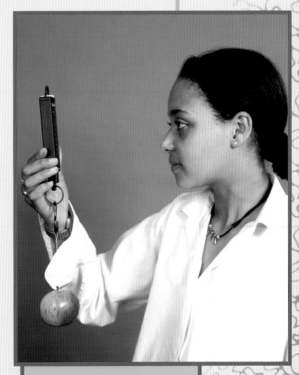

Engineers—people who design and build things—need to constantly check the forces that are involved in their work. Destructive forces, such as strains, can cause machines or structures to fail. In addition to using a variety of instruments to measure forces, engineers use mathematics to model the behavior of structures. They have developed equations that enable them to predict what effects the forces involved in their designs will have.

A forcemeter, or newton meter, measures the strength of weights or other pulling forces. Here, a student weighs an apple, which weighs about 1 newton.

Speed, Velocity, and Acceleration

Everything that moves has a speed. A car might be moving at 65 miles (105 kilometers) per hour, while a person walking along a sidewalk is moving just 4 miles (6.5 kilometers) per hour. Other things, from comets to snails, can be moving much faster or much more slowly.

Speed is calculated by dividing the distance traveled by the amount of time taken. If you ride your bike a distance of 10 miles (16 kilometers) in 2.5 hours, your average speed would be 4 miles (6.5 kilometers) per hour (10 ÷ 2.5 = 4).

These skaters have considerable velocity: They are moving at high speed and are constantly changing direction as they make their way around the rink.

SPEED VERSUS VELOCITY

People often confuse the terms *speed* and *velocity*. A speed is simply a rate of movement. **Velocity** consists of both a speed and a direction. Like force, velocity is a vector quantity. Therefore, 65 miles (105 kilometers) per hour is a speed. Sixty-five miles per hour toward the north is a velocity.

Because velocity includes both speed and direction, a change in either speed or direction produces a change in velocity. An object that keeps moving at the same speed but changes direction can have a very large change in velocity.

A dragster leaves a cloud of smoke from burning rubber as it begins to accelerate away from a stop. For a vehicle to accelerate extremely fast to a high speed, it must use a lot of force.

ACCELERATION

A change in velocity is called **acceleration**. An increase in velocity is called positive acceleration. A decrease in velocity is called negative acceleration or, more commonly, deceleration. When the driver of a car pulls away from a traffic light, the car accelerates, or goes faster. When the driver steps on the brake, the car slows down, or decelerates.

But acceleration does not require a change in speed. A change in direction with no change in speed is also an acceleration. Therefore, a car going around a curve at a constant speed is actually accelerating. That is because a force is required to keep the car moving in a curve, just as a force is required for any kind of acceleration.

NEWTON'S LAWS OF MOTION

The laws governing force and motion were discovered in the 1600s by Sir Isaac Newton. They are called Newton's laws of motion. The three laws explain how forces make objects move or change their speed or direction.

NEWTON'S FIRST LAW OF MOTION

Newton's first law of motion states that an object stays at rest or keeps moving at the same speed in a straight line unless acted on by an unbalanced force. This means that a motionless object, such as a chair, will sit in one place unless you move it. And a spaceship moving in a straight line through deep space will continue that way until something changes its speed or direction.

This soccer player is about to demonstrate Newton's first law, which states that an object at rest (the ball) remains at rest until acted on by a force (a kick).

The first law of motion is sometimes called the law of **inertia**. Mass is not just the amount of matter something contains. It is also a measurement of an object's inertia—its resistance to being moved. If the object is already moving, inertia is its resistance to having its speed or direction of movement changed. That is the definition of mass most scientists use today.

As the amount of matter in an object increases, its inertia increases. You need to exert more force to start a bowling ball moving than to move a marble. Likewise, once in motion, a bowling ball is harder to stop or to push away from a straight line than a marble is.

NEWTON'S SECOND LAW OF MOTION

Newton's second law of motion explains how force and mass are related to acceleration. As you have learned, mass gives an object inertia, or resistance to being moved. Also, a force must be used to accelerate an object—to get a stationary object moving or to change the velocity of a moving object.

Newton discovered that this fact can be stated as a simple mathematical equation: Force equals mass times acceleration. The equation ($F=ma$) tells how much force must be used to produce a certain amount of acceleration with an object of a given mass.

The quantities involved differ from one situation to another. For example, if it takes 10 newtons of force to accelerate a mass of 3 kilograms to a certain speed, then 20 newtons of force would produce twice the acceleration. If the mass were doubled with no increase in force, acceleration would be half as much.

In everyday terms, this equation simply means that it takes a lot more effort to throw a big rock than a small rock. And if you hit two balls of different weights equally hard with a croquet mallet, the lighter ball will accelerate more (that is, go farther) than the heavier ball.

NEWTON'S THIRD LAW OF MOTION

Newton's third law of motion says that all forces occur in pairs. Whenever an object exerts a force on another object, the second object exerts an opposing force on the first object. That opposing force is equal in strength to the original force. This relationship is usually expressed as, "For every action [force], there is an equal and opposite reaction [opposing force]."

If you lean against a wall, you are pushing against the wall with a certain amount of force. The wall pushes back on you with the same amount of force. That does not seem to make sense. But if the wall were not pushing back with the same amount of force, you would break through the wall or knock it over.

Consider a more active force. Imagine that you shoot a basketball toward the hoop while wearing roller skates. As soon as you shot the ball, you would move backward a few inches on the skates. The force you exerted in shooting the ball would produce an equal and opposite force—the ball would push back at you with an equal amount of force. This opposing force would cause you to move backward.

SCIENCE PIONEERS The Genius of Isaac Newton

Sir Isaac Newton was one of the greatest scientific minds of all time. Newton was a young scholar at Cambridge University when he discovered his three laws of motion. At about the same time, he also completed a study of gravity. In addition, Newton made important advances in mathematics and the study of light.

Newton's discoveries about motion and gravity were published in 1687 in a book titled, in Latin, *Philosophiae Naturalis Principia Mathematica (Mathematical Principles of Natural Philosophy)*. This work, usually called simply the *Principia*, is considered one of the most important achievements in the history of science.

But because you have much more mass than the ball, you would move a much smaller distance than the ball would.

Now imagine that you are on roller skates and are holding a lead ball that weighs as much as you do. (For the purposes of this discussion, you have been given considerable strength.) With all your muscle power, you throw the ball. It goes only 10 feet (3 meters) before crashing to the floor. In reaction, you move backward by the same distance—10 feet.

A person who stands on a pair of roller skates and throws a basketball moves backward a few inches. That is because the person is exerting a pushing force on the ball, and the ball pushes back with equal force. This action and reaction demonstrate Newton's third law of motion.

PAIRED FORCES OPERATE ON DIFFERENT OBJECTS

The pairs of forces that operate in Newton's third law do not act on the same object. In both of the previous examples, two different objects were involved. In the first example, the objects were a person and a wall. In the second example, the objects were a person and a basketball. If both the action and reaction force acted on the same object, the two forces would cancel each other out and nothing would happen.

CASE STUDY How Jets and Rockets Work

Blow up a balloon and then let it go. The balloon zooms about the room wildly until it is deflated. You have just demonstrated jet and rocket propulsion. The main difference is that you have used air rather than burning fuel. Newton's third law of motion explains how jets and rockets operate.

Many people think jets and rockets move by pushing on the air behind them. But air is not much to push against, and in outer space there is no air at all. The engine of a jet or rocket ignites a fuel in a chamber that is open at the back. The fuel burns rapidly and produces a large volume of hot gases. The gases exert tremendous force on the jet or rocket. In reaction, the vehicle exerts an equal and opposite force on the gases. If it did not exert such a reactive force, the gases would bore through the wall of the chamber, and the vehicle would not move.

With these paired forces working together, the gases are accelerated through the back of the chamber. In response, the jet or rocket is accelerated in the opposite direction. In much the same way, the compressed air in a balloon exerts a **pressure** on the inside of the balloon, and the balloon pushes back. The air streams out of the balloon, making it into a tiny rocket.

Newton's third law of motion makes it possible for rocket engines and boosters to lift a space shuttle into orbit.

MOTION IN A CURVE

Think of a time when you were riding in a car as it moved around a sharp curve in the road. You felt yourself drawn to the side of the car facing the outside of the curve. Loose items on the seats or the dashboard may have slid in that direction.

What you experienced was the tendency of things in motion to keep moving in the same direction—Newton's first law. No force was acting on the loose objects to make them change direction, so they kept moving ahead in a straight line. Inside the car, those objects—and your body—seemed to be moving sideways. That is because the car was changing direction. Your seat belt exerted a restraining force on you, so you moved only a small distance.

What prevented the car itself from going ahead in a straight line—and off the road—was the grip of its tires on the road. The tires kept pulling the car away from a straight line. The car was constantly changing direction as it rounded the curve. That means that its velocity was changing even if its speed remained constant. Because the car's velocity was changing, the car was accelerating.

Motion around a curve is called **centripetal acceleration**. And the force that keeps a car on the road as it rounds a curve is called **centripetal force**.

UNDERSTANDING CENTRIPETAL FORCE

You can get a better understanding of centripetal force if you think about playing with a ball tied to a string.

If you swing a ball around in a circle above your head, the string keeps the ball moving in a circular path. It does that by exerting a constant pulling force. The force is directed toward the center of the circle, where your hand is holding the string. This inward pull is centripetal force. As long as that force is being applied, the ball will continue to move in a circle.

What would happen if the string snapped? The ball would no longer have centripetal force acting on it. So it would fly away in a straight line from the exact point in the circle where it broke free of the string.

CASE STUDY Centrifugal Force

People often think of centrifugal force as the opposite of centripetal force. Centrifugal force is the force that seems to pull you straight outward from the center of a rotating object. For example, if you are standing on a turning merry-go-round, you feel centrifugal force pulling you toward the outside of the platform. However, this is just an illusion. There is no such thing as centrifugal force. What you feel on a merry-go-round or other rotating object is actually resistance to centripetal acceleration. Your body is making an effort to keep moving in a straight line.

People on a revolving amusement park ride feel as if they are being pulled away from the center of the ride by centrifugal force. But this force does not really exist. The force the riders are feeling is actually their bodies' inertia trying to keep them moving in a straight line.

Momentum

What do you think would be harder to stop, a speeding bullet or a slow-moving oil tanker? If you guessed the oil tanker, you're right. In fact, it would be much easier to stop a bullet than an oil tanker. A thick block of wood would stop a bullet. But even a steel wall would not be able to stop a tanker.

The reason has to do with **momentum**. Think of momentum as the "stopability" of an object. In mathematical terms, it is expressed by this equation: $p=mv$, or momentum equals mass times velocity. (Momentum is represented by the letter p because m is used for mass.)

You can see from this equation that either a large mass or a high velocity will result in a great deal of momentum. A speeding bullet has much more momentum than a thrown rock. However, a bullet has far less mass—and therefore, less momentum—than a huge moving object, such as an oil tanker.

A super-high-speed camera shows a bullet slicing through a playing card. The bullet has very high velocity and therefore considerable momentum.

Momentum that is due mostly to mass relates to inertia—an object's resistance to a change in motion. Inertia increases with mass. So the greater an object's mass, the greater its inertia and the harder it is to stop. A fully loaded tanker has more than 10 billion times the momentum of a bullet, even though the tanker is moving much more slowly.

RECENT DEVELOPMENTS
Guarding Against the Ultimate Momentum

The momentum of an oil tanker moving at the speed of a bullet would be incredible. But space objects called asteroids and comets have far more momentum than that.

A comet is a huge mass of ice, frozen gases, and dust circling the Sun in a very wide orbit. Occasionally, a comet passes through the inner solar system. Asteroids are big chunks of rock that orbit much closer to the Sun.

Asteroids and comets can be massive, and they move very fast. A comet, for example, can have a central core up to 6 miles (10 kilometers) wide. And it can move at speeds of up to 133,600 miles (215,000 kilometers) per hour. A large object from space could wipe out an entire country or even destroy human civilization.

In 1994, after more than 20 pieces of a comet struck Jupiter, the U.S. Congress asked the National Aeronautics and Space Administration (NASA) to start a program to scan the skies for objects that could hit Earth. Astronomers at several U.S. observatories were taking part. An international effort called Spaceguard is also watching for comets and asteroids.

Meteor Crater in Arizona formed when a meteorite struck Earth about 50,000 years ago with the explosive force of an atomic bomb.

CONSERVATION OF MOMENTUM

The momentum of moving objects is conserved, or kept constant. That means that it cannot be lost or just disappear. This is the law of **conservation of momentum**. This law states that any time objects collide, the total amount of momentum stays the same.

When a moving object strikes another object, some or all of the momentum is transferred to the second object, causing it to move. If all of the momentum is transferred, the first object comes to a stop because it no longer has any momentum. At the same time, the second object moves away with the transferred momentum. If only a part of the first object's momentum is lost, then both objects move. But they move with less velocity because the original momentum is now shared between them.

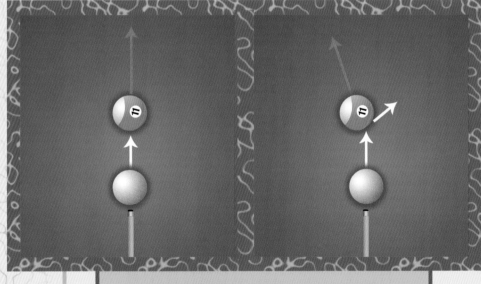

Conservation of momentum can be seen in the game of billiards. When the cue ball—the white ball—hits another ball squarely, the cue ball stops dead on the table. The other ball, having gained the cue ball's momentum, then speeds away. If the cue ball hits another ball on the side rather than straight on, both balls move away in different directions. But they both move at a slower speed than the original speed of the cue ball.

Did you know...?

A golfer "follows through" on a swing when driving a golf ball. That is, the golfer swings the club in a long arc so that the club goes over the person's head and back down again. The purpose of follow-through is to increase the time that the club is in contact with the ball. This enables the golfer to transfer a large amount of the club's momentum to the ball. But even with good follow-through, the head of the club is in contact with the ball for only about one-thousandth of a second!

ZERO MOMENTUM

Moving objects have more than just momentum. They also have **kinetic energy**—the energy produced by motion. As with momentum, the energy of objects is conserved. The main difference is that one form of energy can be transformed into another form. For example, think back to the feature on page 25. Objects from space have a huge amount of kinetic energy. If a comet or an asteroid were to hit Earth, its kinetic energy would be transformed into shock waves and heat.

Two billiard balls heading straight toward each other at the same speed have quite a bit of kinetic energy. Each ball also has considerable momentum. Their *combined* momentum, however, is zero. That is because momentum is a vector quantity. It has a size and a direction. So when two balls are heading toward each other at the same speed, the momentum of one ball cancels the momentum of the other ball.

When those two speeding billiard balls collide head on, both of them recoil, or move sharply backward. That is because their kinetic energy has been conserved. Because they still have kinetic energy, the balls keep moving.

The balls' combined momentum has also been conserved. Because they are now moving directly away from each other, their combined momentum is again zero. Whenever two objects with the same individual momentum are moving at the same speed in exactly opposite directions—either toward or away from each other—their combined momentum is zero.

Bumper cars at an amusement park have elastic collisions, in which objects bounce apart and keep their shape.

TWO KINDS OF COLLISIONS

In explaining the conservation of momentum with colliding objects, scientists talk about two kinds of collisions, **elastic collisions** and **inelastic collisions**. Think of them as collisions in which things either bounce off each other (elastic) or stick together (inelastic).

Elastic collisions take place between hard objects that keep their shape, such as billiard balls. Inelastic collisions involve objects that lose their original shape, such as automobiles that crash together.

In both kinds of collisions, momentum is conserved. In an elastic collision, kinetic energy is conserved. But an inelastic collision results in a loss of the objects' kinetic energy. For example, when two cars collide, they get crumpled. It takes energy to bend and twist metal. The cars' kinetic energy has been transformed into other forms of energy, including sound waves and heat.

Did you know...?

Elastic and inelastic collisions even take place on the scale of atoms and molecules. Atoms or molecules of a gas, for example, move around constantly and bounce off one another. These are usually elastic collisions because the kinetic energy of the atoms or molecules remains the same after the collision. In many cases, however, some kinetic energy is lost after a collision. Such collisions are considered inelastic, even though the atoms or molecules keep their shape and do not stick together.

KEY EXPERIMENT Newton's Cradle

The conservation of momentum in elastic collisions is demonstrated with Newton's cradle, a desk toy with five solid metal balls suspended from horizontal rods.

When one of the outside balls is swung at any given distance and strikes the others, one ball at the other end swings outward the same distance. If two balls swung on one side strike the others, two balls on the other end will swing out. However many balls swing in, an identical number swing out at the other end. In each case, the momentum of the balls is conserved.

Newton's cradle demonstrates the conservation of both momentum and energy.

The Force of Gravity

Think of a time when you watched helplessly as a fragile object fell to the floor and broke. During such moments we are reminded of one of the most basic forces of nature. That force is gravity.

As you learned in Chapter 2, gravity is a force of attraction between all objects based on their mass. Here on Earth, we experience gravity every day. It is the force that causes things to fall down. And it is what keeps us from floating off into space. Gravity is responsible for giving us the air we need to breathe, because Earth's gravity holds the atmosphere around the planet.

Scientists are still learning about gravity. Although they know gravity is related to mass, they are not sure how mass produces gravity. But even though they do not completely understand this mysterious force, they can measure it and predict its effects.

High jumpers attempt to defy gravity. But even the best high jumpers in the world cannot jump much higher than about 8 feet (2.4 meters) before gravity pulls them back down to Earth.

NEWTON'S UNIVERSAL LAW OF GRAVITATION

The relationship between mass and gravity is simple. If mass is doubled, gravitational attraction is also doubled. So a 10-pound (4.5-kilogram) weight experiences twice as much pull from Earth's gravity as a 5-pound (2.3-kilogram) weight does.

However, the gravitational attraction between two objects is not determined just by their mass. It is also determined by how far apart they are. The greater the distance between them, the less the attraction.

The gravity between objects varies in a precise way. To figure how much gravity drops off with distance, simply square the number—multiply it by itself. Then make a fraction out of it. If two objects become twice as far apart, their gravitational attraction to each other becomes one-fourth of what it was. If the objects become three times as far apart, the attraction becomes one-ninth of what it was.

The opposite is also true. If two objects get three times as close to each other, the gravitational attraction between them becomes nines times as strong.

The way that gravitational attraction varies with mass and distance is called Newton's Universal Law of Gravitation. Sir Isaac Newton discovered the law in the 1660s. It is called a universal law because it is thought to be the same throughout the universe.

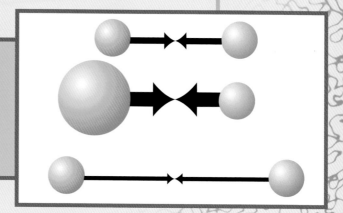

The gravitational force between the middle pair of objects is twice that of the top pair because one of the objects is twice as massive. The gravitational attraction between the bottom pair of objects is one-fourth that of the top pair because they are twice as far apart.

KEY EXPERIMENT Galileo's Falling-Bodies Test

The Italian astronomer and physicist Galileo (1564–1642) was the first scientist to make a serious study of gravity. In the late 1500s, he conducted a number of tests with solid metal balls of different weights. He let the balls roll down wooden ramps in response to gravity and timed their descent.

Galileo found that all the balls took the same amount of time to roll down the ramps, regardless of their size. And the balls accelerated as they rolled down the ramp. Galileo concluded from his studies that Earth's gravity causes falling objects to steadily accelerate in their descent. He also concluded that all objects accelerate at the same rate. It makes no difference how heavy they are. These two findings became known as Galileo's law of falling bodies.

FALLING OBJECTS AND AIR RESISTANCE

You might question the idea, presented in the feature above, that all falling objects accelerate at the same rate. After all, leaves and feathers float to the ground, don't they? They do, but that is because of air. Air does not have much effect on a falling rock, but it has a slowing effect on a falling feather or leaf. This effect is called **air resistance**. Galileo understood that air resistance causes some objects to fall faster than others. Air resistance is a force, because it works against the pull of gravity.

TERMINAL VELOCITY

Skydivers experience air resistance when they jump from an airplane. They accelerate to a downward speed of about 120 miles (190 kilometers) per hour. But then air resistance keeps them from falling any faster. The maximum speed that an object can reach when falling through the air is called its **terminal velocity**. A rock has a much higher terminal velocity than a person because it is much more compact. A rock's compact shape makes it less affected by air resistance.

If there were no air, all objects would fall at the same rate. And they would not reach a terminal velocity. They would continue to accelerate all the way to the ground. The rate of acceleration in Earth's gravity is 9.8 meters (32 feet) per second every second (9.8 m/s^2). That means that every second, the vertical velocity of a falling object increases by 9.8 meters per second.

When dropped through a door in the top of a vacuum chamber (where there is no air) a feather and an apple fall at the same rate. The same would hold true for any objects of any mass.

WHY ALL OBJECTS FALL AT THE SAME RATE

You may wonder why a heavy object falls at the same rate as a lighter object if there is no air. If a 10-pound (4.5 kilogram) weight is attracted to Earth with twice the force of a 5-pound (2.3 kilogram) weight, why doesn't it fall twice as fast?

As you may recall from Chapter 4, one definition of mass is resistance to being moved—inertia. The reason that a heavy object falls at the same rate as a lighter object has to do with inertia. As an object's mass increases, it becomes harder to move. This idea is clearer if we get away from Earth where everything to do with gravity is up and down.

Imagine two objects being held motionless in space near a large planet. Now imagine that they are both released and allowed to move toward the planet, drawn by its gravity. But think of them moving *sideways* toward the planet, like cars on a track. Now it makes more sense that they have to overcome their resistance to movement. The heavier object has more mass and therefore more inertia.

In the mathematics of gravity, gravitational attraction and inertia cancel each other out exactly. For example, an object with twice the mass of another object is attracted to Earth (or any other large body) with twice the force. But it also has twice the inertia of the lighter object. This causes both objects to accelerate at the same rate in response to gravity.

Did you know...?

Ocean tides are caused by the gravitational pull of both the Moon and the Sun. Because the Moon is much closer to Earth than the Sun is, its tidal forces on Earth's oceans are about twice that of the Sun's—even though the Sun has 27 million times more mass than the Moon.

CASE STUDY How Airplanes Defy Gravity

It is pretty amazing to watch a large airliner zoom down an airport runway and rise into the sky. How can something so big and heavy actually fly? Isn't the force of gravity trying to pull it back down? You bet it is.

Defying the pull of gravity is what airplanes are all about. They do it with a force of their own called **lift**. Lift is an upward push on the bottom of a plane's wings that keeps it in the air. But what produces lift?

A main cause of lift is straight out of Newton's third law of motion— every action has an equal and opposite reaction. The wings of an airplane meet the air at a slight angle. The wings push air down. In return, the air pushes up on the wings. The result is lift, and the plane stays in the air.

The force of lift supports the weight of an airliner, allowing it to rise into the sky and stay airborne. Like all forces, lift is a vector quantity.

GRAVITY AND WEIGHT

It is important to understand the difference between mass and weight. Mass is the amount of matter something contains. As you learned earlier, it is also a measure of an object's inertia— its resistance to being moved. Weight is a quantity that is caused by gravitational attraction on matter.

The mass of an object stays the same wherever that object may be—on Earth, on the Moon, or in outer space. Its weight, however, can vary greatly. That is because the pull of gravity on an object is different in different places.

Let's say you weigh 100 pounds (45 kilograms). If you went to the Moon and stood on a scale, you'd find your weight to be about 16.5 pounds (7.5 kilograms). The Moon has about one-sixth as much gravity as Earth, so you would weigh about one-sixth what you weigh on Earth. Your mass, however, would still be the same.

| Mercury: 38 lb. (17 kg) | Venus: 91 lb. (41 kg) | Mars: 38 lb. (17 kg) | Moon: 16.5 lb. (7.5 kg) |
| Jupiter: 236 lb. (107 kg) | Saturn: 92 lb. (42 kg) | Uranus: 89 lb. (40 kg) | Neptune: 112.5 lb. (51 kg) |

You would not weigh the same on the Moon or on other planets as you do on Earth. That is because weight is caused by the pull of gravity, which is determined by mass. Every large body in the solar system has a different mass, so each one exerts a different amount of gravity. The chart above shows what a person who weighs 100 pounds (45 kilograms) on Earth would weigh on the Moon and on other planets.

SCIENCE PIONEERS Albert Einstein: General Theory of Relativity

Sir Isaac Newton showed how to calculate the gravitational attraction between objects. But he had no idea what causes the force of gravity.

The first scientist to develop a theory of what causes gravity was the German-American physicist Albert Einstein (1879–1955). His explanation, presented in 1915, is called the general theory of relativity.

Einstein said that space is much more than just emptiness. He said that space has a fabric, or structure, and that the fabric of space is warped, or bent, by the presence of matter. The greater an object's mass, the more it warps the space around it. Think of a bowling ball that forms a large dent in a mattress. The effect of the bowling ball is similar to what happens in space.

According to Einstein, Earth stays in orbit around the Sun because it is trapped within the warped space around the Sun. Here on Earth, we are pulled down by a warp in space caused by Earth's mass. (In this theory, *space* means all space everywhere, not just "outer space.")

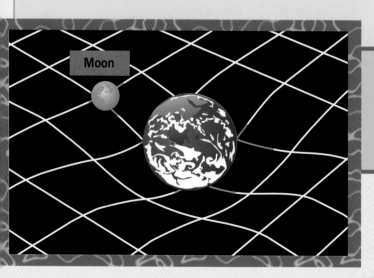

Moon

The lines in this picture are an artist's way of showing space bending around a massive object—in this case, Earth.

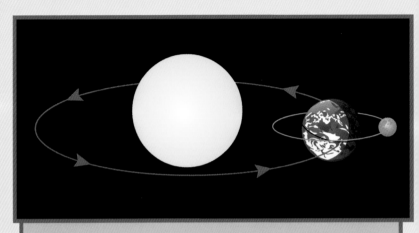

Orbital motion occurs when a moving object is in the gravitational grip of a larger object. Gravity and forward motion are in balance, so the smaller object falls in an endless curve around the larger object. The Moon is in orbit around Earth, and Earth is in orbit around the Sun. It takes roughly 365 days, or one year, for Earth to completely orbit the Sun.

ORBITAL MOTION

Have you ever wondered why the Moon circles Earth instead of escaping into space? Or, on the other hand, have you wondered why the Moon does not come crashing into our planet?

The answer is that the Moon is constantly moving forward and, at the same time, it is held in the grip of Earth's gravity. The Moon is moving in a curve around Earth. This curve is called an orbit. The Moon's forward motion and its attraction to Earth are in perfect balance. For this reason, the Moon continues to orbit Earth endlessly. Earth and the other planets orbit the Sun in the same way.

Gravity provides the centripetal force that keeps the planets and the Moon in orbit. An object orbiting a larger object would move away in a straight line if it were somehow released from the gravity of the larger object. Gravity constantly keeps it from doing that. So the object is kept circling the larger object, just like the ball on the string in the example on pages 22–23. Orbital motion is also known as **free fall**. The Moon is in free fall around Earth, as are the artificial satellites that orbit our planet.

CASE STUDY Experiencing Weightlessness

You've probably seen images on television of astronauts floating around in a space shuttle. The astronauts look, and feel, as if they have no weight. In fact, they still have weight because, even in orbit, they are being pulled by Earth's gravity. But the floor of the shuttle is not pushing up against their feet. Both the astronauts and the shuttle are in free fall around Earth.

Even so, it is common to speak of weightlessness, or zero gravity, in space. And many people wish they could fly aboard a space shuttle to experience it.

For years, astronauts have trained on special jet airliners that produce the feeling of being in orbit. The jets do this by going into steep dives that are close to being free fall. For about 25 seconds at a time, the astronauts float around inside the plane.

Astronauts aboard a training plane experience apparent weightlessness as the plane goes into a dive. Their training plane is nicknamed "the vomit comet" because going into a dive often gives the astronauts nausea.

Did you know...?

Skydivers are said to be in a free fall, but this description is not accurate because they are subjected to the force of air resistance. Only an object moving with no force other than gravity acting upon it is in true free fall.

A cannonball that is shot horizontally from a cannon will hit the ground at the same time as a cannonball that is merely dropped at the same time from the same height. Without gravity, the fired cannonball would continue in a straight line at the same speed.

VERTICAL AND HORIZONTAL MOTION

Imagine that you and a friend are each holding a ball. You throw your ball horizontally (parallel to the ground) with all your force at a certain height. At the same moment, your friend drops his or her ball from the same height. Which ball will hit the ground first? You might guess that the dropped ball will hit the ground first. But, in fact, both balls will hit the ground at the same time.

Horizontal and vertical motion are independent of each other. When you throw a ball, it does not gain any more horizontal speed after leaving your hand. Its forward speed is constant. But it is accelerating downward under the force of gravity. Pulled by gravity, the ball follows a curving path to the ground. At the same time, the dropped ball is simply drawn straight down to the ground by gravity. The downward rate of acceleration due to gravity is equal for both balls, so they hit the ground at the same time.

The motion of the thrown ball is an example of **projectile motion**. A projectile is any object that is propelled forward.

RECENT DEVELOPMENTS The Space Elevator

The pull of Earth's gravity makes it very difficult—and expensive—to get a spacecraft into orbit. A single space shuttle flight costs about $450 million. Engineers have been looking for an easier and cheaper way to get into space.

One incredible possibility is an elevator into space! The elevator would be a huge tower orbiting 22,236 miles (35,785 kilometers) above the equator. It would circle Earth in what is called a geostationary orbit. In this kind of orbit, an object always stays above the same point on Earth.

The elevator tower would be connected to the ground with thin cables made of carbon nanotubes. Nanotubes are a recently discovered form of carbon that are 100 times stronger than steel. Specially designed "cars," called climbers, would zip up and down the cables, carrying passengers and freight. The climbers would move at a speed of about 4,350 miles (7,000 kilometers) per hour. The ride to or from the tower would take about five hours. Spaceships could be assembled in the tower and then sent on missions to the Moon or other planets.

NASA says the space elevator probably won't become a reality until late in the century. But the agency is confident that it will be built.

NASA's space elevator would make it cheaper and safer to send cargo and people into space.

Friction

Let's say you want to move a large, heavy chest from one part of a room to another. You put your hands against the chest and push. What would happen? Very likely, nothing. The chest would not move.

Why are heavy objects often so hard to push from one place to another? One reason, of course, is that they are massive; they have a lot of inertia. But there is also another reason: **friction**.

Friction is a force that opposes the pushes and pulls of other forces. It makes things hard to move. But it is also what makes it possible to walk and to drive a car. If there were no friction, everything would just slide around.

The friction between the head of a match and a striking surface generates heat that causes chemicals on the match head to burst into flame.

Did you know...?

Every surface, even the slickest ice, has some friction. But imagine that you are standing on a completely frictionless surface that goes on forever. Suddenly, someone gives you a push from behind and gets you moving. As Newton's first law of motion tells us, unless some other force comes to your rescue, you will not stop moving. You will continue sliding across that surface in a straight line for the rest of time.

THE CAUSES OF FRICTION

All surfaces have many tiny irregularities, or "hills and valleys." You can see the roughness on some surfaces, such as a sidewalk. The roughness on surfaces that appear to be smooth, such as tile or a polished wood floor, can be seen only under a microscope.

Friction results when the hills and valleys of one surface are pressed into the hills and valleys of another surface. They catch on one another, keeping the surfaces from sliding past each other. This occurs, for example, between your shoes and the surface of a sidewalk. Surface roughness is the most common source of friction.

Even smooth surfaces are rough when viewed under a microscope. When viewed at 50 times its normal size, the surface of polished aluminum alloy shows jagged hills and valleys.

Scientists have learned, however, that there is another important cause of friction called **molecular adhesion**. Molecular adhesion is an electromagnetic attraction between two surfaces. Surfaces have some areas where there is a surplus of electrons, which gives those surfaces a negative electric charge. Those areas repel electrons in the atoms of a nearby surface, causing the other surface to become positively charged. Because opposite charges attract, the two surfaces stick together.

The friction between a smooth surface, such as polished stone, and a "sticky" surface, such as a rubber-soled shoe, is caused mostly by molecular adhesion. This form of friction results when tiny areas of negative charge on one surface are attracted to areas of positive charge on the other surface.

THREE KINDS OF FRICTION

Just as there are different *causes* of friction, there are different *kinds* of friction that we experience when we move objects. Each of these types of friction can be due to either surface roughness or molecular adhesion, though it is seldom just one or the other. But depending on the surfaces involved, either surface roughness or molecular adhesion is usually stronger.

STATIC FRICTION

Static friction is what you experience when you try to push something and it won't move. The word *static* means "stationary," or "not moving." The heavy chest mentioned on page 42 would be hard to move because there is a lot of static friction between it and the floor. The amount of static friction depends on the weight of an object, the material it is made of, and the surface it is on. For example, a wooden crate filled with bricks sitting on a concrete floor has much more static friction than a cardboard box full of books on a polished table.

SLIDING FRICTION

To overcome static friction, you must exert a pushing or pulling force that is stronger than the static-friction force. When you have overcome an object's static friction, it will start to move. But then you have to deal with **sliding friction**. Sliding friction is the resistance to movement of an object that is being pushed or pulled on a surface. But, for the same object and surface, sliding friction is less than static friction. That is because it takes less force to keep a moving object in motion than to get it moving in the first place. However, for many objects, sliding friction still requires considerable force to overcome.

ROLLING FRICTION

Because it can be so difficult to slide heavy objects, people often put wheels under them. It is much easier to roll things than to just push them or pull them, because only a small part of a wheel touches a surface at any moment. It is also easier because the rolling motion of the wheels greatly lessens the effects of friction.

Even so, there is still some friction involved. This is **rolling friction**, the friction between wheels and the surface they are turning on. Rolling friction makes it possible for wheels to function. If there were no rolling friction, wheels would simply spin in place and go nowhere.

REDUCING FRICTION

Friction is the enemy of machinery. Even a small amount of friction can slowly destroy machine parts. The smoothest machine parts have a bit of surface roughness—hills and valleys again. The hills of one surface rub against the hills of another surface it is in contact with. This rubbing causes very tiny bits of metal to slowly get worn away. Eventually, this process causes machine parts to wear out.

Automobiles and many other kinds of machines use materials called **lubricants** to reduce friction. A lubricant provides a protective film that allows surfaces to move smoothly past each other. One common lubricant is motor oil. If an automobile engine suddenly lost all of its motor oil, it would heat up and grind to a smoking halt in seconds.

Friction does not occur only between solid surfaces. When you ride a bicycle, friction from air molecules—the same thing as air resistance— slows your forward motion. Athletes use advanced equipment to reduce friction. Bicycle racers, for instance, ride special bikes and wear special helmets that reduce air resistance.

Pressure

Did you know that air has weight? Well, it does, because it is a form of matter and is attracted by Earth's gravity. Right now, the weight of Earth's atmosphere is causing the air to press down on your body—and everything around you—with a pressure of about 15 pounds per square inch (1 kilogram per square centimeter).

The weight of air is called **air pressure**. We are not aware of air pressure outside our bodies because it is balanced by the air pressure inside our bodies. If our bodies did not have this sort of balance, we would be crushed by the weight of the air.

The weight of air is just one example of pressure, which is a force that we are exposed to everywhere we go. Pressure can be a weight, such as air pressure or the weight of an object pressing down on a surface. It can also be an internal force, such as the air pressure in an automobile tire. In a tire, **compressed air** is exerting an outward force on the inside of the tire.

Pressure is measured in amount of force per unit of area. The unit of pressure is the **pascal**, named for the French scientist Blaise Pascal (1623–62). One pascal is equal to one newton of force per square meter of area.

When a person inflates a tire with an air compressor, the air presses against the inner surface of the tire, stiffening it. The person inflating the tire is also being affected by air pressure: the weight of the atmosphere.

FLUID PRESSURE

The study of pressure usually concentrates on pressures in fluids. A fluid can be either a liquid or a gas. A fluid is any substance that flows freely and takes the shape of a container that is holding it. Both air and water are fluids.

A gas can be compressed to a much smaller volume because its atoms or molecules are not close together. When a gas is compressed, it tries to expand to its previous larger volume. It then exerts great pressure on the inside of whatever is holding it. When you inflate a beach ball, for example, it becomes a stiff **sphere** because the air inside is pushing against the sides of the ball.

Liquids cannot be compressed. Their atoms or molecules are so close together that they cannot be pushed any closer. Because a liquid cannot be compressed, it can transmit a pressure force from one point to another. You can see this whenever you plunge a clogged drain that is full of water.

The ability of liquids to transmit pressures makes them useful for other purposes. For example, automobiles use a liquid called brake fluid. The fluid is contained in narrow tubes connecting the brake pedal with the wheels. When the driver steps on the brake, the braking force is transmitted by the brake fluid to the wheels. There, the force causes the brake pads to press on the brake discs, slowing the car.

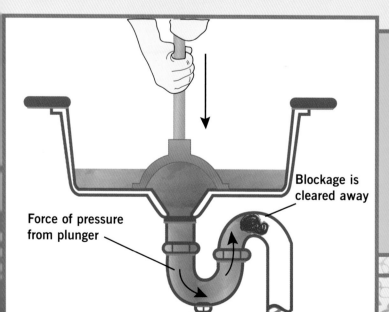

Blockage is cleared away

Force of pressure from plunger

When you use a plunger to clear a clogged drain, the force of the plunger presses on the water. That force is carried through the water in the pipe to the blockage, which is pushed out by the pressure of the water. If only air were in the pipe, the plunger would have no effect.

EXTREME PRESSURES

There are places on Earth where pressures are incredible. One such place is in the deep ocean. Water is heavy, and the weight of water at great depths exerts tremendous pressure. In the deepest parts of the ocean, more than 10,000 meters (33,000 feet) down, water pressure is about 8 tons per square inch (1.2 tons per square centimeter).

The most extreme pressures on Earth are in the center of the planet. There, the weight of thousands of miles of rock and metal, much of it molten (melted), produces incredible pressure. Scientists estimate that the pressure at the center of Earth is more than 50 million pounds per square inch (3.5 million kilograms per square centimeter). This pressure is so great that the iron there is a solid mass, even though its temperature might be as high as 12,600°F (7,000°C)—hotter than the surface of the Sun.

Deep-sea exploration vehicles called submersibles are built to withstand the great pressure in the deep ocean. The most advanced submersibles can descend to depths of more than 19,700 feet (6,000 meters). The pressure at that depth is about 4 tons per square inch (0.6 tons per square centimeter).

Did you know...?

There are some kinds of fish that live deeper in the ocean than the most advanced research submersibles can go. The world's deepest-known fish was found in the ocean near Puerto Rico at a depth of 27,500 feet (8,382 meters). The fish was pulled up in a net that was dropped to that depth.

RECENT DEVELOPMENTS Diamond Anvil Cell

Scientists studying the effects of extreme pressures have an amazing tool called the **diamond anvil cell**, which can produce pressures equal to those in the center of Earth.

The diamond anvil cell works on a simple principle: If a great deal of force is exerted on a tiny area, a tremendous amount of pressure is created. The cell uses two high-quality diamonds that are forced together within a tiny chamber. A very small amount of a material to be tested is placed in the chamber between the surfaces of the diamonds. Then a mechanism is used to push the diamonds together. This puts the material—as well as the diamonds themselves—under enormous pressure.

Scientists use the diamond anvil cell to learn how materials behave in conditions of extreme pressure. For example, researchers are learning how rocks and metals deep within Earth are affected by the pressure there. The diamond anvil cell is also helping researchers understand the basic physics of matter. They can use that knowledge to develop useful new materials.

Diamond is the hardest-known material. But sometimes the diamonds in a cell cannot survive the pressures they are exerting. Many times, the diamonds in a cell have exploded in a cloud of diamond dust.

BUOYANCY

Fluids do not just exert a downward or outward pressure. They can also exert an upward pressure. A helium balloon rises because the air pushes it up. A cork floats in water because the water under it pushes it up.

The upward force that a fluid exerts on an object is called buoyant force, or **buoyancy**. It acts in opposition to gravity. When the upward force of buoyancy on an object is greater than the downward pull of gravity, the object floats.

Buoyancy results from the **density** of different objects and substances. Density is a measure of weight in relation to an object's volume. For example, a block of cork weighs much less than a block of lead of the same volume. Therefore, cork has a much lower density than lead.

Whether a material sinks or floats in water depends on its density in relation to the density of water. Lead sinks in water because its density is higher than that of water. The density of cork is less than that of water, so cork is buoyant—it floats.

In the same way, a helium balloon rises because the helium in the balloon has a lower density than that of air. A helium balloon rises until it reaches an altitude where the air is so thin that its density is the same as that of the helium in the balloon.

Hot-air balloons rely on a gas heater to give them buoyancy. Heat makes air less dense. The burner heats the air inside the balloon, making it less dense than the air outside. This causes the balloon to rise into the sky.

CASE STUDY Floating in the Dead Sea

Have you ever floated on your back in a swimming pool without an air mattress? It wasn't so easy, was it? You had to lie very flat. And you may have needed a lungful of air to increase your buoyancy.

There is a body of water in the Middle East in which it is easy to float. In fact, it is just about impossible to sink! That body of water is the Dead Sea, which lies on the border between Jordan and Israel. It is called the Dead Sea because it is much too salty for fish to live in it. In fact, the Dead Sea is the saltiest body of water in the world. It is about nine times saltier than the oceans.

The high salt content of the Dead Sea makes its water very dense. The high density of the water gives it great buoyant force. That force enables people to float easily.

The Dead Sea lies about 1,300 feet (400 meters) below sea level. With little effort, people can float in the Dead Sea for hours at a time.

Work and Machines

We use the term **work** freely in our daily lives: "I have to get to work"; "It doesn't work"; "It's a lot of work." People define work in different ways—for example, as a task, an effort, or what a person does at a job.

Physicists, however, have a specific definition of work: It is the use of force to move an object in the direction of the force. By this definition, if you pick up a heavy box of books from the floor, you have accomplished work. You applied a lifting force and moved the box upward against the force of gravity. However, if you then carry the box to another room, you have not done any additional work. The force you are applying to the box is still a lifting force, so lugging the box to another room is not work (to a physicist, at least!).

If you left the box on the floor and pushed it into the next room, you would also be doing work. You are applying a sideways force, causing the box to move in that direction against the force of friction. Whenever the direction of a force on an object and the direction in which the object moves are the same, work is being accomplished.

But whichever way a force is applied, it must result in movement. If you push against the side of a box and it stays put, you have not done any work on the box.

Machines, such as this forklift, make work much easier for us.

CALCULATING WORK

The farther you move an object, the more work you have done on it. That is a pretty simple idea, and it is expressed by a simple equation: W=Fd. The amount of work done (W) equals the force exerted (F) times the distance the object is moved in the direction of the force (d).

Work is expressed in metric units called **joules**, named for British physicist James Joule (1818–89). One joule is the amount of work done when a force of one newton moves an object a distance of one meter. (Because doing work involves the use of energy, the joule is also the metric unit of energy.) So if you were to push a box that weighs 100 newtons a distance of 5 meters, the amount of work would be 500 joules.

Did you know...?

Having fun can be work. For example, if you go bowling, you are accomplishing work every time you lift a bowling ball. You are doing even more work when you give the ball a forward force that propels it down the alley. Your work is finished as soon as you release the ball, because you are no longer applying a force to the ball.

In releasing his ball, this bowler has completed work. In another second or two, his ball will meet the pins in an elastic collision.

USING MACHINES FOR WORK

Machines make life easier for us. It is much simpler, for example, to break open a nut with a nutcracker than with your hands. In many cases, machines perform work that would be very difficult—or even impossible—to do without them. Most farmers would not want to give up their tractors and go back to using horse-drawn plows.

Machines are designed to control the size or direction (or both) of forces to accomplish work. With a simple machine, such as a nutcracker or a crowbar, the force is provided by human muscles. A more complicated machine produces its own forces by using energy from electricity or fuel.

THE SIX SIMPLE MACHINES

Complex machines have many parts. But all machines are based in some way on at least one of the six simple machines.

A lever is a bar that is used for a lifting force. A **fulcrum** is a point of support for the lever. When a pushing or pulling force is applied to the bar, the lever pivots on the fulcrum, producing a stronger force. A crowbar and the claw of a hammer are types of levers. A wheelbarrow is also a lever—the wheel serves as the fulcrum.

A playground seesaw is an example of a lever. The fulcrum sits in the center, supporting the weight of the riders.

A wheel and axle is a wheel with a rod, called an axle, running through its middle. The two are connected. When a force is applied to the wheel, it turns and causes the axle to turn as well. A force that causes the axle to turn also causes the wheel to turn.

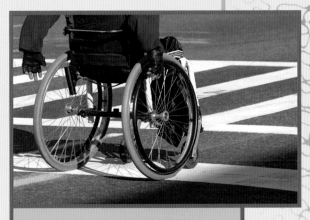

When a person turns the wheels of a wheelchair, the axle that is connected to both wheels also rotates. The result is that the chair, which sits above the axle, moves forward.

An inclined plane is a surface set at an angle—a ramp. Moving something to a higher level by pushing it up an inclined plane requires less force than it takes to lift the object straight up. Moving crews use ramps to load furniture and other heavy objects onto their trucks.

A wedge is a device that slopes to an edge. The head of an ax is a wedge. Wedges are commonly used to sever or split objects by transmitting a force to the edge.

A crane uses pulleys to lift heavy objects. Each pulley attached to the load decreases the amount of force needed to lift the object.

A screw is a shaft with a spiral groove running around it. When the screw is rotated with a turning force, that force is changed into a linear (straight) force. That is why a screw sinks into a block of wood or other material when you turn it with a screwdriver.

A pulley is a wheel with a groove in its surface and a rope or cable passing over it. Pulling down on one side of the rope or cable causes a weight to be lifted on the other side. Complex arrangements of pulleys enable heavy weights to be lifted with a relatively small amount of force.

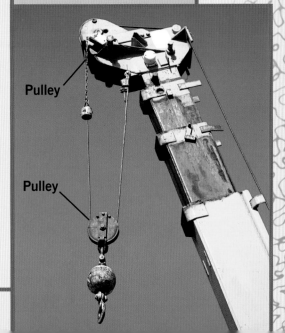

Pulley

Pulley

HOW MACHINES MAKE THINGS EASIER FOR US

Machines allow forces to be applied over a greater distance. That means that a smaller force can be used to accomplish the same amount of work. For example, when you use a crowbar, you might push the bar down 1 foot (30 centimeters) to raise a heavy object 2 inches (5 centimeters). You would be using much less force than if you tried to raise the object with your bare hands. The crowbar has increased the effect of a small amount of force.

This explains why it is easier to push a heavy object up a ramp than to lift it straight up. Less force is required, though that force must be applied over a longer distance. If a ramp is three times longer than the vertical distance, the work can be accomplished with one-third the force. To put it another way, the ramp multiplies a small force by a factor of three.

The amount by which a machine multiplies a force is called its **mechanical advantage**. That number is obtained by dividing the **output force** by the **input force**. The input force is the force applied to the machine. The output force is the force that the machine in turn exerts to accomplish work.

Think again about using a crowbar, and imagine that you are raising a stuck window. Let's say that an upward force of 100 newtons is required to loosen the window. You press down on the crowbar with a force of 25 newtons, and the window breaks free. The crowbar has provided a mechanical advantage of four (100 ÷ 25 = 4).

Simple machines increase mechanical advantage by making it possible to exert less force over a greater distance. The bend near the lifting end of this crowbar is the fulcrum, which enables the crowbar to pry a nail from a block of wood.

RECENT DEVELOPMENTS The Biggest Machines in the World

If you have a tremendous amount of work to be done, you need a big machine to do it. A *really* big machine.

Some of the largest machines in the world are earth movers. Many of these machines are used for strip-mining coal. Earth movers have huge shovels that can lift up to 270 tons (245 metric tons) of dirt or coal in a single bite.

Even the biggest earth movers in the United States are dwarfed by the Bagger 288 in Germany. This monster machine weighs 45,500 tons (41,275 metric tons). It is 700 feet (213 meters) long and 312 feet (95 meters) high—as tall as a 25-story building. The Bagger 288 has a huge rotating shovel-wheel that can gouge away 2.7 million cubic feet (76,000 cubic meters) of soil or coal per day. Now that's doing a lot of work!

The massive Bagger 288 is one of the biggest machines ever built.

What the Future Holds

Scientists are always searching for new ways to harness forces for useful purposes. There are many exciting projects underway that may make the future a very different place.

FAR BEYOND THE SPEED OF SOUND

The best jet engines built so far have enabled planes to fly up to about three times the speed of sound, or approximately 2,100 miles (3,400 kilometers) per hour. But a new jet engine being developed would propel planes at much faster speeds.

This engine is called a scramjet, which is short for *supersonic combustion ramjet*. A regular ramjet engine sucks in air, slows it down, and compresses it. The air is then combined with fuel and burned to produce **thrust**.

With a scramjet, air moves through the engine at the same speed that the plane is flying. When it is combined with fuel and burned, it leaves the engine at an even higher speed. A scramjet engine would enable a plane to fly up to 15 times the speed of sound—10,500 miles (17,000 kilometers) per hour. A plane moving at that speed could fly from New York City to Tokyo, Japan, in two hours. That flight now takes 18 hours on a commercial airliner.

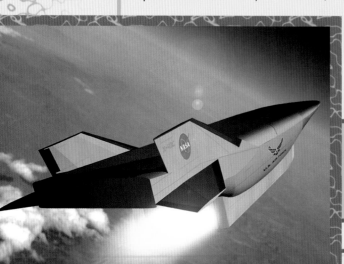

An experimental NASA plane powered by a scramjet engine, shown here in an artist's drawing, might one day set new speed records.

SUPERHUMAN STRENGTH?

Engineers at a number of research centers are working to develop artificial exoskeletons for humans. An exoskeleton is a skeleton on the outside of the body. Many small animals, such as insects and spiders, have exoskeletons.

A human exoskeleton would be a bit like a suit of armor that is powered by a motor. It would enable a person to carry heavier loads and run faster than would be possible without the exoskeleton. Exoskeletons could be used by army troops to make them into "super soldiers." Exoskeletons would also be useful in construction and rescue work.

A nanocar built by engineers at Rice University in Houston, Texas, has four ball-shaped wheels and actually rolls across a surface. In this computer image, each small sphere represents an individual atom. The car is so tiny that 20,000 of them placed side by side would be about as wide as a human hair.

BIG JOBS FOR TINY MACHINES

Engineers are working on devices so small they can be seen only with a microscope. Some of these devices are called **micromachines**. Even smaller ones are called **nanomachines**.

The smaller the size of a device, the less force it can exert. But at these tiny scales, not much force would be needed for many tasks. Researchers are not yet sure what functions micromachines and nanomachines would perform, but they have some incredible ideas. For example, some engineers think it may be possible to build nanomachines that will travel through people's bodies, killing cancer cells and cleaning out clogged blood vessels.

No one is sure just what the future holds for the use of forces. But whatever comes, it is sure to be amazing.

Further Resources

MORE BOOKS TO READ

Angliss, Sarah, and Maggie Hewson. *Forces and Motion.*
New York: Kingfisher, 2001.

DiSpezio, Michael A. *Awesome Experiments in Force and Motion.*
New York: Sterling, 2006.

Juettner, Bonnie. *Motion.* Chicago: Kidhaven Press, 2004.

Smith, Alastair, and others. *Energy, Forces and Motion.*
New York: Scholastic, 2001.

USING THE INTERNET

Explore the Internet to find out more about forces and motion.
You can use a search engine such as kids.yahoo.com and type in
keywords such as **force**, **newton**, **gravity**, **velocity**, **acceleration**,
momentum, or **pressure**.

These search tips will help you find useful websites more quickly:

• Know exactly what you want to find out about first.

• Use only a few important keywords in a search, putting
  the most relevant words first.

• Be precise. Only use names of people, places, or things.

Disclaimer
All the Internet addresses (URLs) given in this book were valid at the time of
going to press. However, due to the dynamic nature of the Internet, some
addresses may have changed, or sites may have changed or ceased to exist
since publication. While the author and publisher regret any inconvenience this
may cause readers, no responsibility for any such changes can be accepted by
either the author or the publisher.

Glossary

acceleration   change in speed or direction

air pressure   force exerted by air

air resistance   force that air exerts on a moving body

atom   smallest complete unit of matter

balanced forces   two or more forces, applied to an object at the same time, that are equal in strength, so that no motion occurs

buoyancy   upward force exerted on an object by a fluid

centripetal acceleration   motion around a curve

centripetal force   force that keeps an object moving in a curved path

compressed air   air that has been forced into a smaller volume, thereby increasing the outward pressure it exerts

concurrent forces   two or more forces that are acting on an object at the same time

conservation of momentum   preservation of objects' total momentum after they collide

contact force (also called mechanical force)   force exerted by physical contact between objects

density   measure of an object's weight in relation to its volume

diamond anvil cell   laboratory device that pushes diamonds together to create extremely high pressures

elastic collision   collision in which the colliding objects keep their shape and bounce off one another

electromagnetic force   force created by the electric charges on protons and electrons

electron   negatively charged particle in an atom; electrons whirl around outside the nucleus

element   substance, such as gold, that cannot be divided into simpler substances

energy   the ability to do work

equilibrium   condition in which all the forces acting on an object are in balance so that no motion occurs

force   push or pull that causes an object to start moving or changes the speed or direction of its motion

free fall   fall of an object that is being acted on only by gravity; an orbit is a form of free fall

friction   force that opposes the pushes and pulls of other forces

fulcrum   point on which a lever rests and on which it pivots

gravity   force of attraction between all objects

inelastic collision   collision in which the colliding objects lose some of their shape and stick together

inertia   the resistance of an object to being moved or to having its motion changed

input force   with a machine, the amount of force applied to the machine

joule   metric unit of work; it is the amount of work done when a force of one newton moves an object a distance of one meter

kinetic energy   energy of motion; the faster an object is moving, the more kinetic energy is has

lift   upward force on an aircraft's wings that enables the aircraft to fly

lubricant   substance, such as motor oil, that reduces friction

magnetism   attractive force produced in some materials, such as iron, caused by the alignment of atoms within the materials

mass   amount of matter in an object; it is also a measure of an object's inertia

mechanical advantage   amount by which a machine multiplies a force

micromachines   machines that are constructed on a microscopic scale

molecular adhesion   type of friction that acts between very smooth or sticky surfaces; it is caused by electromagnetic attractions between the two surface

molecule   combination of two or more atoms; for example, a molecule of water consists of two atoms of hydrogen and one atom of oxygen

momentum   "stopability" of an object; an object's momentum is determined by multiplying its mass by its velocity

motion   movement of an object from one location to another

nanomachines   machines that are so small they can be seen only with the mos powerful microscopes

neutron   electrically neutral particle in an atomic nucleus; *electrically neutral* means it has no electric charge

newton   basic unit of force

nucleus   central part of an atom, composed of protons and neutrons

orbit   curving path of an object circling a larger object in space

output force   with a machine, the amount of force that the machine exerts to accomplish work

pascal   unit of pressure; it is equal to one newton of force per square meter of area

pressure   any force that presses against a surface, such as air pressure or water pressure

projectile motion   motion of an object that is moving both forward from a propelling force and downward in response to gravity

proton   positively charged particle in the nucleus of an atom

resultant force   net force acting on an object that is being subjected to two or more forces; the net force is what produces motion when forces are added together

rolling friction   friction that opposes the forward motion of an object on wheels; it exerts much less resistance than the static friction of the same surface

sliding friction   friction that makes it difficult to push a heavy object across a floor or other flat surface

solar system   the Sun and planets, together with the planets' moons and other objects that orbit the Sun

speed   how fast an object is moving; an object's speed is determined by dividing the distance it has traveled by the time it took to go that far

sphere   object shaped like a ball

static friction   friction that causes an object to stay in place even when a pushing or pulling force is exerted on it; the push or pull is not strong enough to overcome the friction

strong nuclear force   force that holds protons together in the nucleus

terminal velocity   maximum constant velocity reached by an object that is falling under the attraction of gravity

thrust   propulsive force produced by a jet or rocket engine

unbalanced forces   two or more forces acting on an object at the same time that are unequal in strength, so that one force overcomes the other (or others) and produces motion in its direction

vector quantity   measurement that contains both a size and a direction

velocity   measurement that includes both speed and the direction of motion

weak nuclear force   force that plays a part in certain processes by which the nucleus of a radioactive atom decays, or breaks down

weight   effect of gravity on mass; weight increases as gravity increases

work   use of force to move an object in the direction of the force

Index